The Delphi Series
Volume IV

featuring

Ting Gou, Claire Zoghb, & Erin Redfern

Published by Blue Lyra Press

ISBN-13: 978-0692762684 (Blue Lyra Press)

ISBN-10: 069276268X

Blue Lyra Review, a division of *Blue Lyra Press*, publishes three online issues per year (end of **March, June and October**), and a print edition in early spring. We accept poetry, nonfiction, translations, book reviews and artistic images. Flash Fiction is in the month of March & October or by invitation only. Poetry has a rotating guest editor.

Blue Lyra Review considers submissions **Jan. 1 – Sept. 30th**. We accept simultaneous submissions. All submissions must go through Submittable and adhere to the guidelines on our Submissions Page.

Blue Lyra Press publishes every spring and accepts poetry and flash fiction chapbook submissions under 25 pages during the month of July. Send directly to the email below.

Blue Lyra Review & Blue Lyra Press are independent and rely solely on the generosity of donations so **please** support the arts: (**www.bluelyrareview.com/donations/**).

SUBMISSIONS: bluelyrareview.submittable.com/submit

FACEBOOK: www.facebook.com/BlueLyraReview

TWITTER: twitter.com/BlueLyraReview

PURCHASE: bluelyrareview.com/subscriptions/

CONTESTS: bluelyrareview.com/submissions/contests/

CORRESPONDENCE: bluelyrareview@gmail.com

Cover: Aron Wiesenfeld's *The Garden*, oil painting.
Graphic Designer: Claire Zoghb

NOTE TO READERS

Dearest Readers,

If you are returning to this series, then it is quite lovely to see you again and if it is your first book in the series, then it is my pleasure to introduce you to the fourth book in the Delphi Series. This book consists of three separate chapbooks by three separate poets bound in one single volume. Why would anyone do this? Good question! I think you, the reader, picked this book up because you are interested in one of the poets and want to read more of their wonderful work. In doing so, you are now exposed to two other poets. Maybe you heard of them before you picked this book up; maybe you didn't? I encourage you to read all three as they are all superb writers! Besides, it is like getting three books for the price of one!

Ting Gou begins the three chapbooks with two sections of poems that explore the essence of fading and disappearing with a sense of gut-wrenching turns. The opening poem begins with: "When one person wastes away, / The body in the water follows suit. / This is the fidelity of reflections." The reader can't help but follow this elegiac reflection, this poetic journey, where a house and yard are extraterrestrial, where Snow White converses with the huntsman, where even a fading fig wasp holds an aura of beauty. Endings are not endings when they are encased here in these graceful pages.

Claire Zoghb is the next poet in this fourth series. These poems are steeped in the beauty of little moments, those "unseen web(s) holding us aloft". They reveal the universal and thus the exposed world, inviting us to see beauty everywhere. These poems wonderfully walk the boundary between the natural world of skunks, bats and cats, as well as black snails, fiddler crabs, and even a squirrel sutra, to the more urban moments of museums, taxi cab drivers and checkout lines until her "pen cast(s) a shadow / the length of the Nile."

Erin Redfern bookends the fourth series with little lyrical doorways that reveal the wonder of Neverland and Rumpelstilskin, the poetry of time portals and the secret alphabets of birds. All are unique like a poem about sexuality using the metaphor of sugar maple or a little moment in a Girl Scout fashion show that is so much deeper and graceful than we can imagine, poems where you will see the "need to crack the spine, collapse the old leverages.../ blow open the moldering rulebook / by which we abide. We'll engage instead in the guttural wisdom of branches."

So, crack the spine, delve in, and let's prepare to get lost in these breath-taking words. Enjoy!

Full Table of Contents

The Other House

by

Ting Gou

TABLE OF CONTENTS

Part I:
The Other House

A Natural History

When one person wastes away,
The body in the water follows suit.
This is the fidelity of reflections.

Narcissus, the long-limbed hunter,
In pursuit of deer far away from home,
That fatal love already boiling

Underneath his surface,
Slipped into the reeds one day,
Took root, and flowered.

Not knowing this, his mother
Sets her table with purple river buds,
Petals pooling around a vase.

She waits for him. The table bruises.
Red berries erupt from her nailbeds
Like a sickness.

Frankenstein

It's the rotten fruit that buzzes
the loudest. Even the dead

are not shells, become home
for something else. Think of

a fig swarming with larval
bees. Think of your father,

in that house loose shutters
green and white, raving about

penny stocks, lottery tickets,
little machines of the future

with their silver hearts and lungs,
while grass grew so tall,

your mother had to cut it with shears,
stooped forward in that jungle:

Mom as figure in white.
Mom as machete.

And over everything: a heat,
the exothermic tug of a mad voice

pointing you toward the sky: rain.
How you welcomed the severe

thunderstorm warnings for the relief
you thought they promised.

Before the business fell through,
your father scribbled patents,

ate them for dinner. Even the first rains,
which brought nothing

but devastating humidity,
were no setback, and you wonder

if that house, with its insects,
with its dead, was where you learned

to dream, your father sweating through
t-shirts at the cusp of a storm,

talking to no one you can see,
in some trance out of Lovecraft,

negotiating with the dark: how much
for the lightning, how much

for the thing that kills you
and leaves you

unbearably alive?

(untitled)

It starts with the memory of green grass surrounding a white house, the blades against your shins. It starts with apparition. The ghost of a termite infestation, the heatwave of insect wings ascending from ground through which your mother, hunched over vegetation, planted and replanted her legs, huge shears in her hands. It starts with a beheading, the smell of chlorophyll and sap mixed with gasoline. The rubber of tennis shoes. Your mother, young again. You—a neutron star, a forest of jewel-eyed dwarves. It starts with waking from sleep and knowing there was something you forgot to take with you. It starts with trying to reenter the dream, the forest, the house. It starts with moving as if through water toward a door. A little prayer in ink. How the headless stalks swayed like bodies dancing in the foreground of a green and white speckled house, the blades brushing against someone's shins, maybe yours. It starts with the knees of a child.

Excavation: Mobile, Alabama, 1996
After Larry Levis

What happens when you leave
a house?

Its body begins to rot for you
and live on for another.

As much as you deny it,
there are always two houses,

two sets of furniture—
one with refrigerator doors

collecting grime between plastic lips,
new family, new broken-down car

killing the lawn.
Then, there's the house

as you remember it,
swimming upstream

in your imagination, year
after year, consistent as salmon.

That summer, my mother
obtained a box of fish,

their bellies emptied
of caviar.

On the off-ivory counter
by the sputtering garbage disposal,

she intended to make dinner
out of those eggless pouches.

No air conditioning, no job,
no images for our eyes

but burnt grass splayed out for miles
like dirty lace placemats,

houses set in the middle
like cheap teacups.

She deroofed the scales
from spiculated skin,

the supinations of her wrist
calculated and determined,

her gasp sharp and short
when she saw the worms,

pink pencil cores of muscle
sheathing bone,

pockets of activity in the otherwise
dead.

How I've tried to bury it,
the sound of useless flesh

falling into a trash bag.
How I've been drawn to it,

as to a place where something
remarkable happened.

How I stand in that kitchen
and it's me who's opening

boxes and boxes of freshwater fish,
each more terrifying than the next,

looking for what's broken,
what's still alive.

All things rot,
but what happens afterwards?

And who will stumble
upon our remains and ID us,

will they know us from our bones
or the troughs our bodies,

emancipated from substance,
leave in dirt?

Mother, something catches
in my throat, a half-born prayer.

Blessed be the calcified heart,
the mineralized shell

of life hardened in the sun.
The tar that keeps us intact

long enough to be found,
documented, crushed into tea,

no ingredient too taboo
for a mother, a daughter.

Alien

Hello, Heaven. You are a tunnel lined with yellow lights.
from "Yayo" by Lana Del Rey

I'm wading through the grass again,
trying to remember how I got here

and why I'm shivering.
It's raining. My mother is inside

hanging laundry over the bathtub.
The heavy stalks, burdened with new mud,

sink and fold toward each other
over soil involuting

from how my mother's feet struck
the ground as she ran,

our clothes kept dry.
Some time ago, I decided

that this was not
the way to heaven,

though there are yellow lights here too:
rusted gutters blinking white

with lightning,
the neighbor's two-door clunker

screaming in alarm.
Everything oversaturated. No use

for subtle dreams.
The house: a peacock green.

The atmosphere: extraterrestrial.
In this yard where every object

is turning into something alien,
I am being beamed

into a spaceship and I am glad,
think, This is a good thing.

How we can make anything a heaven
by naming it:

Hello, tunnel lined with municipal light.
Hello, house with snakes

in the crawlspace.
And the thought:

had it not been for my father's hand
pulling me back that day

from the hissing coils,
I would still carry the puncture wounds

from a dead animal's teeth.
I'd say I often dream about this house

but that's a lie: there are some things
we resurrect by force.

The lifespan of a house
is the sum of the lifespans

of all its inhabitants.
The aliens, with their technologies,

understand: they know what it takes
to keep from dying.

After a time, we approach
their planet of ice.

The ship starts a mechanical beeping.
Some distant god lifts it dark head

out of the snow.
How close we are all to heaven.

The Other House

Driving home today,
I thought of the other house,

the one loose shutters green and white,
the one panting on the side of the road,

half-dead and someone else's.
Hymenoptera wings encircle a shrub

outside the front window.
A dragonfly crawls in and stretches

its carefully partitioned appendages
in the living room.

It's the version with the upright piano,
the new owners being huge fans

of grossly sentimental movie music,
a piece called "A Song of India"

marked up in pencil on the stand.
A Song of India, meaning there are

multiple songs of India, but this one
was written by a man in a barrack

in St. Petersburg, with city lights
flickering through the snow.

Though sometimes I visit this house
and it's empty,

only the single dragonfly or bee
resting on the wall, licking itself.

Call it *A* Version of Emptiness then,
because with the insects there

I'm not alone.
It's amazing how even the dead,

inside their shells, hold such life.
In the backyard, the viridian excess

of a vine wrapped around a utility pole
is a bird taking to the air,

is steam rising from pavement,
is green, steady smoke

leaving the scene of a fire.
Did I forget to tell you

this is also the version
where I'm outside, where I'm six

or maybe seven,
inventing the perfect game

with my imaginary sister. It's called
Pretend You're at the State Fair,

and you're lying on your back
on a huge wheel.

Someone on the ground grabs on
and runs.

The pendants and blinking bulbs
above you spin, and you stare

at their naked faces. At some point,
we are all drunk on light.

Part II:
Surviving Winter

Snow White explains to the huntsman the material of his prison

Not glass. The glass was for the girl
who's gone. Though sometimes,
I am curling my fingers
around heartstring. I am holding an ax,
its neck unyielding in my palm.

Brother, you tell me you killed a man.
I don't ask how
his life left in front of you
and for that I'm sorry.

What leads us to the forest
one could imagine
won't save everyone.

Brother, I mean to say
my face was too much for you
to bear.

Later, your hands glowing
in boar's blood,

you pocket the queen's gold
but don't remember
how you got there.

Some things you leave to die
in the yellow ground.

Brother, the game will kill you.

Brother, you're crumbling.

To draw poison from the snake,
you must unhinge its jaw

and let it bite.

The poison will dissolve flesh,
burning as a myth does
to get out of
its shell.

The Fig Wasp

Think about the sweetness,
that purple sanctuary.
This is all a male, wingless,
will ever know. Sugar that drips
from his sisters' bodies.
The wax world, a dense heart
of which they are the heartbeat.
Hold the right fig to your ear
and you can hear the universe
swarm with larval wasps.
And isn't he, at least, pitiable,
that even after being born,
this little honeyed bell is all he knows?
And what mythology does he invent
to explain a life so dark and sweet?
When you left, I would imagine
you inhabiting doorways.
And for a year, how the light caught
the hairs on your arm.
Hold the right fig to your ear
and hear everything.
The male fig wasp bores a hole
through the hardened fruit for his sisters.
They escape and multiply.
He crumbles in the sun.

Landscape in which the world is ending

Because the world will be swallowed in your sleep,
your brother grows taller in the other room
& your sister takes someone into her mouth,
sprouts feathers, becomes wild.

All summer long, you find the bucktoothed skulls
of furless voles under beds, over kitchen cabinets.
You & your sister both understand
there are some things you do not speak.

The family navigates through its hunger.
The skulls keep appearing like mushrooms.
You scoop them into your palms,
marvel at their emptiness, their weightless earth.

Landscape with prophecies

It will be the hunted things
that save you.

Your brother will build a city
from a pile of crooked teeth.

Years later, your sister will be married
& you will stumble upon your brother's city on a map
& on some days you will find your breasts
cupped in the hands of a stranger.

You will drink from half-closed mouths
& find between your teeth
pieces of your brother's city,
strands of your sister's hair.

You will retreat into a cabin.
You will make the woods haunted.
You will hear someone is looking for you.
No one will be looking for you.

Landscape in which your sister is missing

In the other room,
your sister coughs up bones

when she thinks you're not listening,
but being an owl yourself,
you're always listening
& hear everything—

the window sliding open,
the mechanics of her wings clicking,
not unlike your wings,
the soft pellet scratching against her throat.

Even later,
as you undress her forbidden room,
prepare her things for disposal or donation
in a house devoid of forest creatures,

you listen still
for the *tic tic* of tiny ribs against lacquer.
You talk to her, a little.
You unbury the ghosts of mice.

How to Survive the Winter

Find a warm coat, a pretty face.
Sculpt the white landscape

into the startling pin turns
of a sea monster's spine.

This proves you are not blind.
There is something

beneath the ice.
Breaking through the snow

like a shipwreck,
like the green and black throat

of a bird dead
on the laundry room floor,

feathers splitting light.
Far from knowing

how it got here,
you're not even sure

how you got here,
but some mornings with cold stars

over your shoulder
you walk by the river

and leave a trail of crumbs
for the sun to follow.

Heavy with ice, the trees
strip down to a lattice

of bare branches where light
gathers like crows,

the only thing that moves.
You don't know

the exact mechanics of how
an animal crumbles to its knees

in a snowstorm or what bones
populate the ground afterwards,

only that there are fifty thousand
species of fungi

and what eats at us
does so methodically:

eyes, marrow, tendon.
And the bird in the laundry room

keeps pinned to its skin
a brooch of brilliant feathers,

the last ornament to break down
on a body killed by the cold

or what still grows in it.
You've seen enough death to know

that funerals are for the living,
but you cover the torso anyway

with a dryer sheet.
In winter, a strange language

blooms on your tongue,
turns broken trees

raking their branches through the river
into broken men

panning for gold.
As any doomed settler,

you worship each shining thing
as a sign that the land,

despite its anger,
will save you:

it's hard work
raising the dead.

The seeds you grip
are double-coated, fossilized.

You dig only shallow graves.

How to Tell You're Still Alive
Saginaw, Michigan

You wake up with four legs,
your skin an accordion of tendon and bone.

Maybe you've finally made it,
or maybe you're a horse.

Not the poor kind with sad, round eyes
tethered to a flea market circus,

five dollars for a ride, three for a picture,
but the kind with finely architectured sweat

and rugged barn musculature,
by which I mean

please imagine the shirtless back
of a young man of your choosing.

The kind that says, *I am alive, a horse.*
The kind that says, *Aren't you ashamed*

of fences?
North of here, by Walloon Lake,

steam pours out of the nostrils of a child
and becomes the half-moon ankles

of ponies chasing each other's necks:
red roan, cremello, fleabitten gray.

Such incredible ice keeps us
from setting ourselves on fire

and I truly believe we won't die
at the hands of ghosts either,

though there are knives growing out of us
the way lightning grows out of the ground

when it strikes.
If we are each the fantasy

of someone,
then the world is filled with horses

that used to be human.
And your owners?

They bring you sweet wine
and sugar cubes to suck,

by which I mean
please imagine the hazel eyes

of a creature worth selling everything
to keep alive.

No shame for fencing you in.
Your owners feel no guilt.

Not even when the barn rots
and collapses in the middle of winter,

twists your spine into a fist,
because it's their fists

underneath the rubble, their bodies
housed beneath your skin.

This is where I leave you,
with all your little knives.

You have consumed everyone near you
and like a star exploding

you die for the thousandth time.
It won't be your last.

Someone will bring you back.
The snow puddles around you.

You become an island,
a soft neck, a sun.

You give off tremendous heat.

Disaster Survival Guide

The summer brought so much rain,
when the power went out,

I became an island.
I had no candles, only books.

I opened the blinds and shuffled around
by moonlight.

Of course, the electricity was gone for days,
and I became populated by owls

and strange reptiles.
Soon, ships started landing

with lost astronomers and poets.
We tried to draw ourselves a map,

but ended up writing ballads
about our lovers back home.

Many animals were charmed by our songs
and named us their gods.

And like gods,
we appeared to them in visions

as dreamers drowned
in gold dust.

On the fifth day, the power came back
and the star-gazers were gone

but the poets stayed.
The moon lost its gleam

and the deer became mute two by two.
After the storm,

we quantified the damage,
put out the electrical fire

in the yard across the street.
In the new dark,

we renamed all the planets
and the stars we wished into orbit.

What happens next:
we won't disappear.

There will be rumors
about us.

The neighbors will write stories
about a people fashioned

out of wind and lightning,
and if they don't,

we will write them ourselves,
tell posterity about the time

when everything was on fire—
even the ocean was burning—

but it warmed us
from a distance.

Acknowledgements

My immense gratitude to the following journals in which these poems, some of which in earlier forms, appear:

Arcturus—"How to Survive the Winter";

Best of the Net— "The Fig Wasp";

Ghost Ocean Magazine— "Snow White explains to the huntsman the material of his prison", "The Fig Wasp", "Landscape in which the world is ending,", "Landscape with prophecies", "Landscape in which your sister is missing", and "Alien";

r.kv.r.y.— "Excavation: Mobile, Alabama, 1996";

Superstition Review— "A Natural History", "Frankenstein", "(untitled)", and "The Other House";

Word Riot— "How to Tell You're Still Alive".

Biography

Ting Gou is an M.D. candidate at the University of Michigan Medical School, interested in psychiatry and the relationship between memory and identity. Her poems have been nominated for the Pushcart three times and appear in the *Bellevue Literary Review, Best of the Net 2014, decomP, Ghost Ocean Magazine, Midwestern Gothic, r.kv.r.y., Superstition Review, Word Riot*, and elsewhere.

Boundaries

by

Claire Zoghb

TABLE OF CONTENTS

Skunk

What is left but this: The compulsion to tell.
                    – Mary Jo Bang, "The Role of Elegy"

She was but a rustling at first—
a crinkle of dried rhododendron leaves
under multiple feet. I rushed to the window
to see, spinning under the blue moon's light,
an armful of white-and-black-striped cotton candy.
Three baby skunks rolling one another in the grass
while their mother swept enough leaves
to disguise the burrow she'd dug beneath
our sunroom. All business, she then led them
to the lawn in search of grubs.

For weeks I watched the nightly procession, the mother
so sure of herself—even after only two babies followed her.
Yet she got into the rat poison put out by the neighbors.
How many days she suffered, or where her
offspring were, no one knows. She made it back
home, her bloated body wedged in its entrance
pulled by the gentle gloved hands of the wildlife guy.
He photographed her, *per state law*, before he slid her into
a black plastic bag for *disposal*. A few spadesful of soil
squirming with maggots into another bag and it was over.
He left her burrow lightly blocked (in case of survivors)—
a standing brick topped with a cement shard, looking like
a Neolithic tomb. Yesterday's turned-up earth pales
in today's stronger light, growing grayish,
her stench of rotted
onions already dissipating under a new season's sun.
And found curled in this morning's grass—three nests
of white fluffy hairs, holding perfect circles of dew.

Night Flight

The plane noses its ascent through clouds visible
only when we're inside them and I wonder if this
is what dying is like—climbing the sky, alone
among neat rows of strangers, all holding
their breath, as I do, or praying, or simply awaiting
the signal to reconnect with life: to place ears to cells,
soles to carpet. Legs extended from our spaces,
narrow and assigned, so little room at our sides
we need to cross our arms on our chests. Below,
the world lies flattened, simplified by distance.
Untethered, we leave the living behind, to their glittering
cul de sac bracelets, opera-length strands of interstates,
and the dark velvet spaces between, our ties to the
earthbound
an unseen web holding us aloft.

The Bat

with a line borrowed from Adrienne Rich

Separate beds were the rule
in your parents' Vermont cabin.

So after we'd fooled around enough
one of us would stumble three feet

to the other double. Once, unable to sleep,
I noticed movement high on the wall,

a stir of wing. Not wanting to startle it
into flight, I balled up a sweatshirt,

lobbed it at your head, hissed
There's a bat on the ceiling.

You rolled over, then panicked,
shot to your feet and ran in circles

as the bat flapped, frantic to escape.
Lights snapped on at the stairs.

Your father appeared in boxers,
wielding the kitchen broom:
Bats fly in figure eights!

If I dream of you at all these days
I recall how moments of quiet bliss

turned upside down, how we flailed,
blind and unarmed, in the face of a wildness

we knew next to nothing about
swooping down upon our heads.

Devotion

It's not that his lips crave
the earthly texture

of Grecian wood, the scent
of pigment or broad crinkled

expanses of gold leaf.
It's more that he's forgotten

how to touch his wife.
She lies in bed, stripped of her paint

and gilt, and holds her breath
as he performs his daily devotions:

each morning and before retiring
he finds it simpler to kiss

the forehead of his patron saint
depicted with great wings,

head in hand.
She knows he'll never

sprout wings or golden halo
despite his faithful reverence

of icons written by men
clustered on holy Mt. Athos

as she awaits the miracle
of his kiss,

the nights, the years,
growing like splinters

beneath her nails.

Open Letter to a Cairo Cab Driver

You aimed your dented cab at me.

The small flame of my bare head
must have drawn you,
my pale Western skin wrapped
like a mummy in linen
despite the summer heat.

I still see the rusted grille,
your ancient teeth, laughing.
Your tin *hamsa* swung from the rearview mirror,
but what would protect *me*?

There to view your country's antiquities,
I forgot about you once inside the museum,
taken by Tutankhamun's treasure—
galleries of alabaster, silver and turquoise,
his golden death mask.

Where are you are today
now that cabs no longer circle Tahrir Square?

On the rooftop, hurling bottles of fire
onto those risking everything
for better lives?

Or rubbing shoulders with freedom
in the streets, in the white winter light,
whipped by men on stolen camels?

Perhaps you were simply bored
that scorching afternoon eleven years ago.

But know this—I saw you. I saw *you*.

Italian-Honeymoon Haibun

A chic trench cinched at her thick waist, our city guide
steers us through St. Peter's immensity. A small tight flock,
we shuffle after Albertina, pointing the way with her
umbrella, raised and unopened, through the Basilica's half-
light. Through a school of Buddhist monks in saffron robes
flashing like koi. Through scent of candle wax and
centuries, of Carrara sunshine clinging to marble. She
guides us past the pallid agony of the Pietà to the writhing
muscular columns of the baldacchino, created by this
miniscule nation's genius builder. *Bare-knee-knee*, she
makes us repeat after her. *Bare-knee-knee*. Pausing
beneath a pale Teresa, orgasmic with pain or love,
Albertina grasps one of my husband's glossy black curls,
stretches it taut in her overripe fingers:

Come Sansone...
I needed no translation
from this Delilah.

Prayer

In Cleopatra The Baths District, Alexandria

Day ripens. Melon scent rises in the kitchen, mixes with the tang of iodine blowing off the sea. Vendors on donkey carts have come and gone, hawking honeydews, shouting for scrap metal. Each song echoes, settles into the street's ancient dust. It is the hour of pigeons. Yours will soon return, banking over the Corniche. I watch the city slow. Downstairs, the baker locks his shop for the night. I nod to the boy on a balcony across the street, call out a greeting in my most precise Arabic. He answers in English, says his name is Mohammed. I tell him mine, ask his age. *Khamsa.* Five. We taste the juice and salt of the foreign words on our tongues.

Only five months
since the towers crumbled
and we can speak.

Afghan Warrior

He rises before you from over the ridge—

His rolled *pakul* shades his black almond eyes
a tangle of beard sparse as the brush between these rocks
He carries Alexander and Genghis Khan in his DNA
tangled with generations of grandfathers taught
by every passing army how to deal with invaders
He carries a Kalashnikov like you held a Camel
those days you rolled your own: without thinking
He is the January wind biting through the Hindu Kush
He carries the Koran in his memory, letter by letter
Nothing covers his fingers against the ice
He knows how to tangle with invaders like you—

He will give you just enough time to call on your god.

Katyusha

Katyusha *is a wartime song about a girl longing for her beloved and the name of a multiple rocket launcher first used by the Red Army during World War I. The rockets make a distinctive moaning sound in flight.*

Trailing a white ruffled sash
it flies due south

casting a shade
across the Galilee
so brief
no one notices.

Slender-waisted maiden
in a cloudless azure dress

how is it I know *your* name

and not the name
of the first man you meet

he, at midday rest
in the orchard
green almonds
slipping
from his gnarled hand
eyes closing on a dream:

his wife as a girl
among sheep like clouds
at rest on the hillside
her *khimar*
the exact shade of the sky
she walks into

her name
a distant music on the wind.

Flower

In memory of Fadwa Tuqan,
poet of the Palestinian people

All it takes
is a white flower
crushed
into a girl's hand
by a boy with shy eyes

and a brother to notice

for doors to close,
windows to shutter.

But there is another brother

inside the dark rooms
who teaches you to weave
a chain of words so long
it can be thrown from the window
across the courtyard
over the fountain
into the mouths of the world.

In the Checkout Line at the Health Food Market

Against the blackness of the Hasid's suit
a single *Iris sibirica*—

wrapped in a clear plastic cone
like a long green paintbrush

brilliant blue-violet in the bristles,
dabs of white and gold at the tip.

I set more mundane items on the conveyor—
raw almonds, brown rice—and wonder

what makes the color of flowers so intense.
I want to ask him. But I sense a border

between us, his black fedora more exotic
than the iris. White strands of his *tzitzit* dangle

down black trousers toward shoes so pristine
they look wet. So I say nothing.

All my life I've waited for permissions:
hall passes, green lights, visas.

I've been awed by those
who don't wait, who may

or may not beg forgiveness,
dazzled even, by their daring

as I am dazzled now by the way
this bright afternoon paints

the parking lot he now crosses,
holding the flower upright

as if about to dip it
into the white-yellow sun.

The Lion of Panjshir

*For Ahmad Shah Massoud, assassinated by bin Laden's
agents two days before the 9/11 attacks*

You've the look of a savior in your fine bones.
I mistook you for Bob Marley on the book's cover.
Your Tajik hat could have held piles of dreads.
But it's a Kalashnikov in your long brown fingers.

I mistook you for Bob Marley on the book's cover.
Perhaps you *were* a musician. Before the Soviets came.
That Kalashnikov in your long brown fingers?
Its inventor dreamt of poetry before the Nazi invasion.

Perhaps you *were* a musician—then the Soviets came
And the soundtrack of your life became small-arms fire.
Its inventor dreamt of poetry before the Germans invaded;
Now your men all hold his work in their mountain hands.

So the soundtrack of your life became small-arms fire—
What else do you do, when life intrudes on your dreams?
Now your men all hold AK-47s in their mountain hands.
Bob sang *Every little thing gonna be all right…*

What do you do, when life invades your dreams?
Your Tajik hat could have held piles of dreads.
You promised the people: *Every little thing gonna be all
right…*
You've the look of a savior in your fine bones.

Boundaries

We're treading dangerous territory, my father and I,
in this cool room, on the hottest day of the year.

He stares out at the towering hickory
he tends dutifully when it sheds

its green segmented nuts. Five times a day,
he sweeps up the shards the squirrels

leave behind.
He confuses Hamas with Hezbollah.

But they're all the same, aren't they?
And we all know Arafat robbed his own people.

As for the Jews? *They were getting roasted in Europe,*
he shrugs. *They needed a home.*

Simple as that.
I have not stood in the places he has—

on the damp bricks of the Auschwitz crematoria,
the silken dust of Jerusalem's streets.

He marvels at Israeli technology
capable of detecting and bombing Gazan tunnels in just the
right spots;

I marvel at the lengths people will travel
to feed their children. Outside in the steamy

late afternoon, his garden flourishes.
Cabbage leaves large enough to wrap his head.

Zucchini runs riot over the broccoli,
stealing its light. Spilling over the fence,

so many succulent tomatoes
he cannot stake them fast enough.

Should someone show up in his backyard to declare:
This land belongs to us *now*

I know what his answer would be.
So I listen. Hold my tongue.

Gulf

For Fouad

When heat prevented you from keeping doves
you loved a cat instead. She claimed you at
your office door, rubbed her bones
against your pants. You walked on streets that float

on top of sand, loafers sinking deep
into the day contained within cement.
To whom did she belong, if not to you?
Khamsin about your ankles. Devil of dust.

Translucent as *kamarudin,* the desert sky
now gentles towards evening while—their sands
already cooling—dunes slide across
the roads to reassemble themselves there.

Dubai

khamsin: a dry, hot, sandy local wind, blowing from the
south, in North Africa and the Arabian Peninsula

kamarudin: sun-dried apricot paste

Aïda

Vermont Studio Center

It's Open Studio Night, but Aïda is not speaking.
Sifting down her pale calves, piling at her toes like Sarajevo snow,
Fine brown powder, redolent of mothers and mornings.
Her shoulders shimmer in an ivory chemise.

Sifting down her pale calves, piling at her toes like tonight's snow,
Coffee, falling from a brass grinder in Aïda's chilled hands.
Her shoulders shiver in an ivory chemise.
Does she look for the future in her daily grounds?

Coffee falls from a brass grinder in Aïda's chilled hands.
She marks her days on frosted paper squares.
Does she still glimpse the past in her daily grounds?
She walked out of one of the past century's last wars.

She marked each day on frosted paper squares with
Fine brown powder, redolent of mothers and mornings.
She walked out of one of the last century's last wars.
It's Open Studio Night. Aïda does not speak.

Boys on a Beach

In memory of four members of the Bakr family,
murdered by the IDF on July 15, 2014 on a Gaza beach

What sights do you look through
that you no longer recognize a small boy
stretching his legs
disobeying his father's warnings
to stay off the beach?

You do not disobey.

How do you, the man, no longer feel
the boy playing inside you?

Mohammad, 11

Boys playing hide-and-seek.
They could not hide from you.

Ready or not, here I come!

Your shell finds the first boy,
explodes the fisherman's hut.

Do you, the soldier, no longer seek
the man hiding inside yourself?

Ismail, 9

Your sights are state of the art.
They see boys scattering.

Through whose eyes do you gaze
when you fire the second shell?

Zakariya, 10

Smoke clears—
three more boys
scattered in pieces
stretched across the beach
for their mothers to gather.

Ahed, 7

The whole world looks to you,
seeking a soldier,

finds something else.

A Squirrel Sutra

inspired by the Heart Sutra

Oh, white-bellied rodent, acrobat of high
branches, commuter of treetops, your eye
and mine catch on a small flame of red.
A cardinal, glowing, standing like a king
in view? The squirrel sees before I do:

No scarlet bird is this, but a nest of thread
or string. Look, there is blue yellow
green twisted round those branches, too.
He tears toward the colorful mess,
begins to tug, throwing his full winter
weight into the struggle. He pulls and

the clump separates. Distinct squares appear,
strung together: Buddhist prayer flags!
The banner gives way. No regard for the words
printed there, with intuitive wisdom, the squirrel
stuffs the cloth petitions into his mouth

leaving both arms free for the sprint home
along the crowded highway of branches, gray
as his back, to his immaculate repository of
cast-off, stray things, where he will spread
the rainbow in his teeth as an added blessing,
and sit, victorious in its center, meriting all praise.

In Wellfleet Harbor

Scores of fiddler crabs flee my approach—
    a single sideways exodus I register
        only after each outsized claw

tucks deep into mud—leaving me alone
    at this brackish edge,
        wind loud on my face.

Jains wear a muslin veil over their mouths
    to protect the teeming insect souls
        from death by inhalation.

But what of the unseen spider,
    crushed beneath the bed-pillow,
        the gnat swallowed with the tea?

I hear through my heels
    a pulsing beneath the sand—

I harm
    as surely as I stand
        here in this harbor

the whole world in motion,
    vulnerable in its flux:
        cirrus wheeling in silvery shades,

tide receding with the light,
    and as it ebbs,
        seagrasses bow their glossy strands

over colonies of black snails,
    exhaling clouds of mosquitoes
        as they lay themselves down.

In the Cairo Museum

So many towering things
in that dusty country:
pyramids, columns, obelisks
and three-story Pharaohs,
one granite leg extended
as if to crush us.

A relief, then
these seated scribes
lining the museum's glass shelves—

small enough to fit the palm,
legs akimbo, a kind of love
in the hunched shoulders,
tiny hands poised mid-glyph,
each stylus lost to the ages.

Egyptian by birth,
monumental in his own way,
my father-in-law was silent
as any stone Ramses.
He would not speak to me
for half a decade.
Yet, that May afternoon
in those airless halls,
the dynasties fell away
with the sound of his voice.
Clara, come see—
they mummified their cats.

Fouad has lived seven years
in his own tomb now.
I smooth fresh scrolls
of papyrus across
my alabaster knees,
head bowed, waiting,

my pen casting a shadow
the length of the Nile.

Acknowledgments

823 on High: "Afghan Warrior"

Blue Lyra Review: "Skunk"

Crab Creek Review: "Boundaries"

MEZZO CAMMIN: An Online Journal of Formalist Poetry by Women: "Aïda" and "Prayer"

Naugatuck River Review: "The Lion of Panjshir" and "In the Checkout Line at the Health Food Market"

PrimeTime Cape Cod Magazine: "A Squirrel Sutra"

Rufous City Review: "Devotion"

Sukoon: "Open Letter to a Cairo Cab Driver" and "In the Cairo Museum"

"Night Flight" was a Semi-finalist for the 2011 Rita Dove Poetry Award.

"The Bat" was a Finalist for the 2011 Rita Dove Poetry Award.

"Italian-Honeymoon Haibun" appeared on the blog, *The Gloria Sirens*, 2014.

"Afghan Warrior," "Katyusha" and "Flower" were chosen as winners in the 6th Annual Nazim Hikmet Poetry Competition and appear in the 6th Annual Nazim Hikmet Poetry Festival Chapbook.

"In the Checkout Line at the Health Food Market" was selected as a Finalist in the 5th Annual *Naugatuck River Review* Narrative Poetry Contest.

"The Lion of Panjshir" was selected as a Semi-finalist in the 2nd Annual *Naugatuck River Review* Narrative Poetry Contest.

"Boundaries" was chosen for Honorable Mention by Dorianne Laux in the 2011 *Crab Creek Review* Annual Competition.

"A Squirrel Sutra" won Third Place in *PrimeTime Cape Cod Magazine*'s 2008 Writing Competition.

Biography

Claire Zoghb's first collection, *Small House Breathing*, won the 2008 Quercus Review Poetry Series Annual Book Award. A chapbook, *Dispatches from Everest*, is forthcoming from Fomite Press. Her work has appeared in *Connecticut Review, CALYX, Crab Creek Review, Mizna: Prose, Poetry and Art Exploring Arab America (The Lebanon Issue)*, and *Natural Bridge*, among others, online at *Sukoon, Mezzo Cammin: An Online Journal of Formalist Poetry by Women*, and in the anthologies *Through A Child's Eyes: Poems and Stories About War* and in *Eating Her Wedding Dress: A Collection of Clothing Poems*. Claire was the winner of the 2008 Dogwood annual poetry competition and one of the ten finalists in the 6th Annual Nazim Hikmet Poetry Festival. Her poem "Terminal" has been nominated for Best of the Net. She works as Graphics Director at Long Wharf Theatre.

Spell Breaking and Other Life Skills

by

Erin Redfern

TABLE OF CONTENTS

Secret Alphabet

The book squawks, lays three blue eggs,
and the red-headed cranes stretch their necks
to bend their black legs. Watching their knees,

we remember how things that look backward
just move a different way. The cranes laugh,
and the rain writes its secret alphabet

on the surface of the lake. They chortle,
and poppies bend their stems, their fuzzy pods
showing the seams, listening for each other's

waking. Petals are bound wings,
after all, as are curtains. Without houses,
all the windows would take flight. Double doors

spread their feathered panes, opening back and back.
A small girl weaves her brown wings in a braid
down her back and closes her eyes. She knows

how doorways work, how words dropped on a lake
reveal its name, how to fold paper into bird
shapes, how wings drip their dark ink when it rains.

Sugar Maple

I stood splayed, mute, leafless, trying to root
in a fallow sky. Underneath, he tapped
me dry. At first I welcomed the slow plunge
and twist, my amber juices flowing toward
the wound like spring. When I gave out he bored
again. He used no bucket, just his tongue
lapping, then thrust up the spouts, hard, as sap
drew back into its freeze. My residue
smeared across his mouth and chin, the sweet grains
in sticky clots off which, stubborn, he still
tried to feed. And if I lived, he would kill
me with these appetites. And so I died,
or seemed to, a dark-crusted, dormant bride
with unborn leaves that moved inside like flames.

Scared Moon

The hallway unrolls its dry tongue in the dark,
swallows you past lintels to stand
before the sink's cataract gleam. Meet the mirror's
blank eye. Take your hands from your face,
expose the black hole where your nose
used to be. It's caved in, or torn up, or rotted off,
or all three. A scared moon beats its wings
against clapboards and shutters. In feathers
it falls down the wall, on the mat.
The shower stall splits in the glass. The center
gapes. You cannot take your hands away.
Under your fingers, it's blacker than sin. Cold
porcelain breathes your nightgown thin,
tiles click and crusty silver hinges
chitter for their prey. In your sleep your true face
grew its nothing on the face you used to be.
These hands, their broken hinge, your frozen gaze.
Where will you go? How will you live?
Who will love you now?

Frogger

1.

don't turn around, know
from the muffled thumps
on the grass back there
that frog is still after you--
wet and frankly amorous
crasher of tea parties,
pounder against shut doors,
bibulous croaking sac with
flapping, mottled tongue--
a splotchy bookmark
that wants its place in you.

2.

she woke with her tongue
croaking hoarsely in her mouth,
an amphibian bloat
nesting between her jawbones.
how would she eat? but then
she caught a fly for breakfast.
talking proved more difficult:
in a rasping chirrup she asked for
coffee, change, affection
and the dessert menu. people
ignored these indiscrete
requests, their hands
waving her words away
like flies.

3.

negotiations get you nowhere
but listening, night after night,
for damp slap on stone,
for splayed, sticky fingerpads
moving blindly along the bedframe,
for low modulations
lisped through the pillowcase,
tadpole whispers
that swim you ear's meatus,
flagellating like mad
as they crowd and wriggle
into their legs, lay
eggs of their own.

4.

the spindly legs
would crack like matchsticks
on the backswing: she might
drop him on herself, so in the end
she cupped him almost gently,
cradling the clammy purse of him
while his pulsing throat grew
against her palm, and hurled
him toward the open door. she missed.
when morning entered the room
she could still hear him
dripping down the stones,
his entrails strung like an argument.

5.
no more gowns and golden balls,
only the bleak rule
of her future: this book.
after some deliberation
she kept the offended hand,
evicted that ventriloquist
tongue, whose progeny
she pulls out by the roots.

she watches pages flip
under her thumb, blurred
sentences bouncing, burying
themselves in the margins'
white drift. words
hop off the page, kick
silently away. punctuation
floats and bumps
like pool toys in the blank
—–-inflated, inarticulate—
black eggs that cluster
and won't hatch now

Precipitate

He had it in the bag.
He could have drawn
the string. Instead
he capered around
an open flame
while the fledgling queen
tried and failed to guess
his name. Big mistake.
"Rumpelstiltskin," she says,
and he stamps one small foot
straight through
the polished marble floor.
(Who among us hasn't
known this rage?)
He has to haul himself out
while her courtiers laugh
tears into their eyes.
Back at his cottage
in the woods he cooks
a thin stew, tipples
air that tastes of smoke
and rue. The campfire flares
like a heart, spits on
her triumph, his shame:
he has only himself to blame.
He might have known
supersaturation of elation
precipitates ruin.

Neverland

Who isn't Peter Pan?
Who wants to grow up,
and never have a mother?
Who isn't Tinkerbell
with her tiny, furious wings,
stamping her little foot,
screaming, "You silly ass!"?

Who isn't a Lost Boy,
so far from home?
Who isn't Wendy? Who wants
to let motherless children
stay that way?

Who isn't the mermaids,
combing and combing their long hair
for a silly boy's attention?
Who isn't the ship, sitting at anchor
with every sail unfurled?

Who isn't Hook, and a handshake
is never simply a handshake?
Who isn't the hook, beckoning
what it will impale?

Who isn't the alligator?
Who hasn't swallowed time
and carried it full in the belly?
Who isn't the clock?
Who hasn't heard herself ticking
and wondered who she will be
when the bomb goes off?

Unblocking the Fifth Chakra in a Dream

clogged drain
rusty and dank
my throat grown
pipe-wide

I can reach
inside, pull out
dead-blonde hair
in clumps, caught

pencils and flapping,
back-bent books, then
the red ribbons
float up, luminous

against clotted
dark, rippling
through what blocked
the way

all that crap
that wouldn't go down
no matter how many times
I swallowed

Reality Check

after Jane Hirshfield's "I Have No Use for Virgins"

I have no use for theories.
Give me the press of roots, the buckle of sidewalks,
and bare feet feeling their way in the dark.

Manicurists, goat farmers, welders, cashiers--
let many men and women on this idea bus
before it's careening driverless toward a sea cliff.

I'll be the guardrail.
You be the air suspended
over crashing waves of truth.

Lonely Only

I wish I could spin around so fast that when I stopped,
I'd have a new name.
                    Bethany Schultz Hurst,
                    "Crisis on Infinite Earths", *Issues 1-12*

A lonely only, I
used to wish
for a best friend. I
prepared for her, knowing she could
appear in anyone, suddenly, like a spell, or a spin
and flick of a godmother's wand. I left clues around:
heart necklaces already jaggedly split so
I could bestow the "Best" half, folded letters sealed fast
with melted wax, misspelled lemon-ink notes that
bloomed when
held close to a bulb, alphabet codes even I
could barely crack, locked diaries that came with two tiny
      keys. (When I stopped
to try them, all the keys opened all the diaries, so I'd
stash them in separate places.) I was president of secret
            friendship clubs that didn't have
any members yet, or even a
secret. I wrote her into stories: long-lost sisters reunited,
            off on new
adventures. Pacts. Villains.
When we got separated, her brave voice calling my name.

Out of a Blue Room

Father's Day 2015

It just happens sometimes.
We are easy together, then we aren't.
Phones turn into plastic and wires

while our hearts kick away underwater.
We are talking, then I'm in a blue room.
It just happens sometimes--

while our hearts kick away underwater
I am always six, and alone,
hitting and holding my stuffed bear.

We are talking, then I'm in a blue room,
hitting and holding my stuffed bear,
my voice falling to the carpet

with the sudden gravity of dead wings,
the space between us filling with plastic and wires.

To find a doorknob, wake it from an old, old sleep,
to walk out of a blue room into my life

with my voice buried in the carpet back there--
even now it can take a long time. But
I'll remember about doorknobs, remember how to get
          me out

you'll come through the window if you have to.

Does your room also fill with the sudden silence of
          dead   things?
Maybe it's not a room.

Maybe it's an endless balance beam you have to cross,
a sequence of handstands and round-offs
you must execute even though you don't know how.

Maybe it's a tree giving its leaves away,
trying to pass for a mailbox,
which will just eat anything a person feels like feeding it.

Maybe it's a balance beam.
Maybe it's a sorry tree.
Maybe it's a grease fire,
and the only words you have are made of water.

While you scour the pantry for a bag of flour,
I'll remember about doorknobs
and walk out of a blue room.
Maybe it's not a room.

Loose the bag of flour--
it will send up white dust like vengeance
and settle like regret.

We were easy together, then we weren't.
Even now, it takes a long time
to find a doorknob, wake it from an old, old sleep.

You don't have to walk on your hands forever.
You don't have to pass for anything else.
You don't have to give away all your leaves
or eat anything you don't want to eat.

White dust rises like vengeance,
then settles the fretful fire.
I am always six, and dreaming.

The only words we have are made of water.

You'll come through the window if you have to,
even though you don't know how.

Patti Finds a Time Portal in the Forest of Nisene Marks

Her husband hiked ahead, turning
just enough to be heard. *Goddammit,*
you're just going to have to learn to keep up!
Beyond the stubbled set of his jaw, she sees
her son glance up, then away, and *the vacation*
could have been over like that her thumb and
        middle finger
snap. But something else happened, some strange
sea-fog magic or fair folk spell, some bay-scented blessing
        everything
got big and slow--redwoods sloughing their sun-struck
        dust,
the trail breathing, his mouth shaping the words, the words
themselves moving sluggishly through air
like slow-motion movie bullets, so slow
she could hear them twice, once in present time,
once forty-seven years ago: her husband a boy
tow-headed and tired, his pack somehow heavier
long after lunch. The line of scouts, a khaki tail
disappearing, *flick,* round the far bend in the trail,
and the Scoutmaster's voice, his father's voice
silencing juncos and jays, lobbed back for him to catch
like an apple, or a grenade. When the portal closes,
she carries the remains of that other place--
cobweb coating huckleberry bush, banana slug
dragging its sticky clump of duff, patches of sorrel
contracting in sun, and her son, her husband
skirting the far ravine--two unexpected flowers
in the middle of all that green.

After Kentucky

walls of the wooden house tick
man cuts coupons at the sill
while brown leaves slip between the boards
late too   late to save what needs
        bathing beauties copper pennies orders
           to report his hungry heart

whiskey snicker of pinking shears
sends moths through the room
wings curl in the heat powder the walls
        the curtains where they
he has to go over each receipt each leaf each wing
crumbled to a drift of varicolored dust
how to breathe   in cracking heat
        and silt of years

so hot waiting for Jesus to come
planning the past saving their defoliated sons
and the ones that came out kicking
        kegs and forties down a dirt road yeah he's got
girls pink pinafores took the oven knobs
and his sucking teeth with them
        married wars of their own

he hasn't gambled since a long afternoon
in that small back room her baking
in the sun-backed door   his ticket punched, pulling
        at her apron strings

guest soaps crochet hooks let-out hems
pails filled with black hawk berries recipes
        stitched in code stuffed
in the batting   crazy quilt
she wasn't telling him
        something making him finger the knotting
           unable to work only
               tighter for the tugging

now he makes for her sewing basket
fills his mouth with buttons thimbles all those things
he wanted to throw away
        be free of and not bitter

she went to get more once and was gone
rolled dough, crimped crust gone black
smoke fluttering to pine   black hawks
        staining the countertop pie
                still raw in the middle

Mean Jolene

Mean Jolene has bees in her chest
and a honey-stuck throat. She loves a cracker-jack
whiz kid, hates to explain herself.

Mean Jolene works in a dusking room.
Her red pen otters through rivers of prose.
Words, words--rash paddlers she bobs
with an inky tip before turning on her back
to crush and munch a tender mussel.

Mean Jolene loses two minnows in the shallows,
five gold coins to ebb tide. Come semester breaks
these currents are stronger than you'd think;
rafts just sink and boats with passengers
won't float. Can we blame her
for striking sweetly, for saving herself?

Mean Jolene loves Huck better than Jo,
thinks only some tides are worth the wade.
If she works hard and does what she's told
maybe her lost minnows will swim back to her,
maybe coins can be flesh and blood again.

Mean Jolene somersaults the red pen,
locks me homeless in hallways.
She's left something precious under her desk,
curl of a girl who wants to go home,
minnow-lost little who has no home but this.

Girl Scout

The whole troop volunteered for the fashion show.
It was 1958. Her father drank.
Her mother had been sick since always. God
made her brother smart, so what could she be
but good? Not-quite-good-enough girl
who couldn't bear the thought of being on display.
At rehearsals, scouts were put through their paces.
The day before the show she took the dog
for a walk. Beneath madrones and bays
the light was soft, the woods hushed.
They strayed into a thicket of poison oak.
Parting the thornless canes, wriggling farther in,
feeling the shade-cooled air on her sun-browned skin,
she hid her face in the blushing leaves again and again.

Kaitlin

If a casserole, surprise layer of potato chips.
If a potato chip, able to hold a disproportionate amount
        of salsa.
If a proportion, as divine as that of the leaf, the nautilus,
        the curling edges of grief.
If a nautilus, one that whirls the dark deep with its own
        jet propulsion.
If a jet, one that hasn't been built yet.
If a building, a rambling house with a secret attic, short
        staircases, alcoves stashed with essentials:
        driftwood, rocks picked up on solitary walks,
        sentences strung like necklaces from their hooks.
If a rock, not a geode, but one in which the quartzy veins
        have traveled up to the surface, following their own
        mineral argument.
If a traveler, one with a soft-sided suitcase.
If a suitcase, one that floats when the ship goes down,
        sustaining its owner until the Coast Guard arrives.
If a ship, one with dark flags from the lands you have seen.
If a place, the city you can hear when you're in the deep
        end, the city on the other side of the grate, the grate
        to which the key has not been made.
If a key, the one that fits its own lock
perfectly.

Marita

She'd rather be at a pool party:
I can see the turquoise dream behind her eyes,
their floating gaze corralled by serious
amounts of kohl liner. Earlier today
she sailed through the lunch break,
her mouth a bright toy turning
in every flirtatious breeze. Now faded
by an afternoon's exposure to problem sets
and student-led discussion groups,
it drifts and bumps against her chin.
Frankenstein sits on the desk between us,
a heavy goose that won't lay. She sighs.
The brief mascara flicker when she finds
that Godwin was her own age
when she bedded Shelley and brought
her creature to life can't save
this one stillborn afternoon. Twilight
approaches; she and I pick our way
across Walton's Eurasian tundra,
featureless as this overblown Norton edition.
(Do we really need one more khaki cover,
one more perplexing introduction
to stall the cumbersome caravan
before it rolls out?) My rucksack's
stuffed with rations; hers displays its slack
like a flag of surrender, the canvas tongue
flapping with the sound sandals make
smacking the warm surface of a wet pool deck.
I'll throw her a Slim Jim. She'll sigh
again. Anytime, anywhere, anyway,
she'd rather be at a pool party.

Boom Box

Remember how many batteries a beach trip took?
I could sling the strap of my bubblegum pink
boom box and carry it like a purse.
Two decks to make mix tapes, but mostly
I used it when something good came on the radio,
not even looking up from homework spread
out on the carpet, recording over last week's
hits until the cellophane strip was a palimpsest
of pop voices and Top Gun guitar riffs.
Remember how good we got at guessing
when to stop rewinding so we could hear
that song from the beginning, that A side single
someone bought the whole tape for? There's no
such thing as fast-forward anymore, no time
for hyphenation. So that when I find a stack
of old calendars, the looped scrawl is a stranger's.
Who was this girl who scheduled driver's ed classes
and summer league games, who slipped
her slim sense of self into relationships
like tape decks, pretending the B-side songs
could be as good, wanting to be belted out
like arena rock, listening only for a backbeat
she could dance to, as though synched motion
were commensurate with being understood?

Poem for Paavani

I hear you're pouring pain
into shot glasses, drinking
it down, getting it out of the way.
   Don't be a Jane.

Jane is an endangered species
   in a leopard-print bikini. Jane
is high heels on black ice,
   a ripped seam dripping its batting.

If I could go back, I'd stop
   the local news crew
photo shooting you stripped
   of all you'd done, dumbed down

high school senior: baby-blue shadow,
   pink Barbie lips, teased hair,
girl-body doll-dressed in satin
   short-shorts, skimpy slut-jock wear.

I remember the click
   of your pen, your cold-cock eyes
when I pushed you to write
   freshman year. You pushed back,

then did better. Don't be a Jane.
   Bang a war drum, break glass,
smash temples, tear down the frame.
   Kick, little lickspittle,

hit back, bend rules, buck
   the trend. Swipe two black
war stripes to cancel the glare. Sight,
   speak from the hip. Dare to mind

your beautiful mind.
   Call your shots. Tend

your rage. Take up space.
Keep. Stay. Mend.

Where There's Smoke

nose so cold when she'd kiss me
home from a late night meeting
tired, sober, raincoat soaked in smoke
skin, hair smelling of smoke
it filled the hollow tented coat
when she leaned
                              over me,
cotton mound that wanted to be
a princess, a ballerina, pretty
something mothers love
waiting for it to happen
for the wand to wave
for the spell to be broken
waiting for goodnight and smoke
and an icy-nosed kiss,
for the clasp of long cool fingers
she'd untwist the last one
from my fist, turning toward
the lit doorway, leaving me

a hollow newly scooped
waiting for the next cold kiss
like a rain barrel waits for rain
always emptied too soon
leaking to boot, but all the same
knowing she came in
by the smell of smoke
where the air had been

Going Numb

*You are neither here nor there, / A hurry through which known
and strange things pass*
        --Seamus Heaney, "Postscript"

In September the dark yew places are nearer, the roses
       harden their hips,
and the light, humbled, approaches sidelong and hungry
      as a cat,
so that you know even the sun frets over these half-turned
      leaves,
this mist exhaling from the neighbor's dryer vent,
this face you turn to the sky, or to the ground at your feet,
asphalt sticky with oil, slick-fuzzed with pollen.

In the Target parking lot someone dropped six batteries
between the blades
of the African Iris, and by the curb an empty plastic
Duracell wrapper,
its edges feathered where it could not be torn and was
forced.
I gathered these toxic fruits, their capped heads,
wondering at the urgency of cameras and Nintendo games,
thinking of the value of flowers, ground water, the lungs
and fur of moles,
their extra thumb--we all level up in our way.

 Can we help our porous beings through which so many
      known
and strange energies pass? We're reading the carpal tunnel
      signs,
we're bequeathing our defibrillators and hydraulic jacks.
We need to crack the spine, collapse the old leverages.
Santa Ana, we invite you--—blow open the moldering
      rulebook
by which we abide. We'll engage instead in the guttural
      wisdom of branches,
trade bone marrow's insider tips, track the exchange rate of

tubers,
hum along to the city's nerves going quiet, going numb.

Acknowledgments

Grateful acknowledgement is made to the editors of the following journals in which these poems first appeared:

Blue Lyra Review: "Boom Box";

Bryant Literary Review: "Precipitate";

Clementine Poetry Journal: "Unblocking the Fifth Chakra in a Dream";

Foliate Oak Literary Magazine: "Kaitlin," "Marita";

Heron Tree: "Secret Alphabet";

Marathon Literary Review: "After Kentucky," "Patti Finds a Time Portal in the Forest of Nisene Marks";

Perfume River Poetry Review: "Where There's Smoke";

Porter Gulch Review: "Poem for Paavani";

{Prong & Posy}: "Mean Jolene";

Red Wheelbarrow: "Frogger";

SLAB: "Scared Moon";

Two Cities Review: "Sugar Maple";

Xanadu (Long Island Poetry Collective): "Going Numb";

Yellow Chair Review: "Girl Scout".

Biography

Erin Redfern works as a poet and writing mentor in Silicon Valley. Her poetry has been nominated for Best of the Net by *Crab Fat Literary Magazine* and *Blue Lyra Review*, and she is a 2016 winner of the Poetry Society of America's Robert H. Winner Memorial Award. In 2015 she co-edited Poetry Center San Jose's print publication, *Caesura*, and she is serving as poetry judge for the San Francisco Unified School District's Arts Festival 2016. www.erinredfern.net

Critical Praise

Ting Gou

What portion of our selves is made from remembered images we can't shake? Ting Gou's poems work in searing scenes, with steel and economy in their quick, wrenching turns. *The Other House* marks the debut of a brilliant new poet. —**Susan Wheeler**, author of *Assorted Poems*

Claire Zoghb

The poems in *Boundaries* wander through the vulnerable world in search of what connects us. Written with intimacy and attuned to the differences that foster empathy, what I like is how these poems do not suppose answers for suffering but instead invite me to look outward, to look up from the page and take notice of what's around. At this short collection's core is a reverence for life amid conflict, and a sense of wonder that lives beyond the words. – **Dorianne Laux**, author of *Awake* and *Book of Men*.

Erin Redfern

"Petals are bound wings"—and thus the lyrical brilliance of this compact collection confides with the forthright efficacy of a "how-to" manual for surmounting life's most relentless obstacles. Everywhere, there are doors through which one must trespass, vocabularies dissolving in water, and flaming mishaps of monumental proportions to bypass. Erin Redfern, with her radiant images, has captured in these frank and gallant poems an earnest search party in the rescuing of our strayed and much-necessitated selves. –**Cynthia Schwartzberg Edlow**, author of *The Day Judge Spencer Learned the Power of Metaphor*.

In Erin Redfern's new chapbook, it is full of fresh, intimate bouquet of poems, a fearless persona connects the visceral and the mythical, the vegetable and the sexual in vivid close-ups and poignant echoes. Hallways with tongues, tadpoles that whisper, "air that tastes of smoke and rue," and much more magic weave the reader into this collection. –**Lita Kurth**, writer & co-founder of Flash Fiction Forum

About the Editor

M. E. Silverman is editor and founder of *Blue Lyra Review* and Review Editor of *Museum of Americana*. He is on the board of *32 Poems* and is a reader for Spark Wheel Press. His chapbook, *The Breath before Birds Fly* (ELJ Press, 2013), is available. His poems have appeared in over 85 journals, including: *Crab Orchard Review, 32 Poems, December, Chicago Quarterly Review, North Chicago Review, Tupelo Quarterly, The Southern Poetry Anthology, The Los Angeles Review, Tulane Review, Weave Magazine, Many Mountains Moving, Pacific Review, Poetica Magazine* and other magazines. He is co-editor of *Bloomsbury's Anthology of Contemporary Jewish American Poetry* with Deborah Ager, and he is co-editor of *Warning! Poems May Appear Longer than They Appear: An Anthology of Long*-ish *Poems* with Andrew McFadyen-Ketchum (September, 2017). http://www.mesilverman.com

www.ingramcontent.com/pod-product-compliance
Lightning Source LLC
Chambersburg PA
CBHW071330130626
46556CB00004B/1837